Sir [illegible]
(1[illegible]
Philosoph[illegible]math, Poet
and Playwright*

Peter M. Dunn,

MA, MD, FRCP, FRCOG, FRCPCH
Emeritus professor of perinatal medicine
and child health, University of Bristol, UK

*Presented to the Bristol
Medico-Historical Society,
December 11th, 2017

© Clinical Press Limited 2018

All rights reserved. No part of this publication may be reproduced, stored in a retrieval system, or transmitted in any form or by any means, electronic, mechanical, photocopying, recording or otherwise, without prior permission of the copyright owner

The right of Peter M. Dunn to be identified as the author of this work has been asserted by him in accordance with the Copyright Act 1988

While the advice and information in this book is believed to be true and accurate at the time of going to press, neither the author, the editor, nor the publisher can accept legal responsibility for any errors of omissions that may be made. The publisher makes no warranty, express or implied, with respect to the material contained herein.

Published in the Controversy Series by:
Clinical Press Ltd., Redland Green Farm, Redland, Bristol, BS6 7HF, UK
in association with the Bristol Medico-Historical Society as a supplement to the Society's Proceedings Volume Eight.

British Library Cataloguing in Publication Data
History: Bacon, Sir Francis. Shakespeare, William

ISBN 978-1-85457-095-6
Sir Francis Bacon

Dedication

To my dear and long-suffering wife, Judy, who has for more than two decades allowed our home to be cluttered with my Baconian library and papers.

Preface

The request to speak about the life and times of Francis Bacon following a Christmas dinner of the Bristol Medico-Historical Society presented more than one challenge. For a start the audience would be replete and ready to doze.

Then Bacon, a remarkable and multi-talented man of great industry, had lived for sixty-five years throughout the reigns of Elizabeth and James I, a time of dramatic changes, many influenced by himself. Moreover, because of his birth Bacon, who loved mystery, had cloaked many aspects of his life in anonymity and secrecy. At the same time he left a trail of clues as to the truth that he hoped future generations would eventually unravel. This indeed has been the fascinating project in which I, and others, have been engaged for many years.

The key to Bacon's life is that he was, I believe, the illegitimate son of Elizabeth I by Robert Dudley. Once grasped, then much else falls into place. Furthermore, among his many achievements Bacon was, I am convinced, the true author of the plays and sonnets that we currently attribute to William Shakespeare.

In the time available I decided to state baldly the conclusions I had reached regarding Bacon's life and times. There was little time to present the evidence in support of what I said (and have written) and no time to debate the counter arguments. Much of what I said remains controversial and I have to confess that in places I have made assertions represented as matters of fact, that are based on my interpretation of the events and people involved.

For those who may be offended by my dismissal of the much admired and loved William Shakespeare, I apologise. For sixty-five years I too believed without question that he was the greatest poet and playwright of all time. Alas, the truth that he was just a "non-de-plume" will, I believe, be increasingly recognised as the years go by.

The challenge of long-held beliefs whether philosophical, religious or historical, often arouses deep emotion and attracts severe criticism. All I can say is that after many years of study the views I have expressed are sincerely held. And as Bacon wrote: *'If a man will begin with certainties, he shall end in doubts; but if he will be content to begin with doubts, he shall end in certainties'*.

Schopenhauer once wrote:
"All truth passes through three stages. First, it is ridiculed. Second, it is violently opposed. Third, it is accepted as being self-evident."

PMD

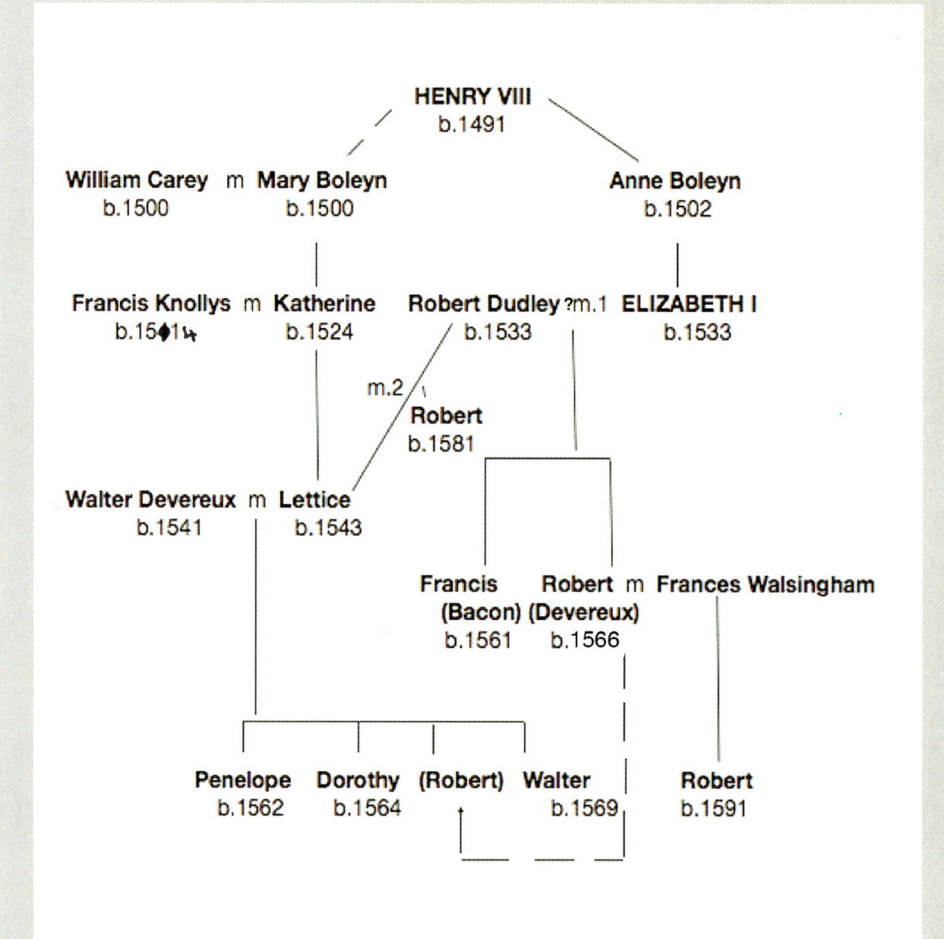

```
                          HENRY VIII
                           b.1491
                         /         \
William Carey  m  Mary Boleyn        Anne Boleyn
   b.1500         b.1500              b.1502
                     |                   |
Francis Knollys m Katherine   Robert Dudley ?m.1 ELIZABETH I
   b.1514        b.1524          b.1533           b.1533
                          m.2 /  \
                             / Robert
                              b.1581

Walter Devereux m Lettice
   b.1541        b.1543

                      Francis   Robert  m  Frances Walsingham
                      (Bacon)  (Devereux)
                      b.1561    b.1566

Penelope   Dorothy  (Robert)  Walter        Robert
 b.1562    b.1564              b.1569       b.1591
```

**Frontispiece:
Henry VIII's offspring by Mary and Anne Boleyn**

Sir Francis Bacon
Philosopher, Polymath, Poet and Playwright

Cast your mind back to the death of Henry VIII in 1547. In the last half of the 16th century England with a population of four million, was emerging from the medieval period. It was a time of great religious dissention and almost continuous warfare with France, Scotland, Spain and Ireland. Taxation was high and disease and poverty rampant. Censorship was severe and punishment brutal. The language of the intelligencia was Latin. Most of the population, perhaps 90%, spoke a primitive English and were illiterate. Actors were regarded as little better than vagabonds and upper class poets and playwrights often deliberately concealed their activities and works.

The conventional history of Elizabeth's reign contains many distortions, illusions and myths. As Elizabeth herself wrote:

> *I grieve and dare not show my discontent,*
> *I love and yet am forced to seem to hate*
> *I do, yet dare not say I ever meant*
> *I seem stark mute but inwardly do prate*
> *I am and not, I freeze and yet am burned*
> *Since from myself another self I turned*

In 1996 I bought a book on the life of Sir Francis Bacon, written in 1981 by a serious historian, Jean Overton Fuller (Fig 1).

Reading it I was astonished to learn from her that Elizabeth I was by no means a virgin queen and had

Fig 1
*Cover from Jean Overton Fuller's book
'Sir Francis Bacon', published in 1981*

had two if not three offspring. One of these, Francis Bacon, was born in 1561 and fostered by her Lady of the Bedchamber, Anne Bacon. Anne was the second wife of Nicholas Bacon, Keeper of the Seal. Furthermore, Fuller stated that Francis in later life had, using a pen name, been the true author of the "Shakespeare" sonnets and plays.

I found these claims so extraordinary and hard to believe, that I decided to research them for myself and that is what I have been doing for twenty-one years. In that time I have read several hundred books on the subject and recorded many thousands of references. For me, it has been a fascinating voyage of discovery. And what is my conclusion? It is that Fuller's claims are justified as near certainty as one can state. Further I discovered that Jean Fuller was not the first to make these claims. An even better account with similar conclusions on Bacon's life was published in 1949 by Alfred Dodd, a Shakespearean historian. I can also strongly recommend Dodd's 1938 book on *'The personal poems of Francis Bacon, (our Shakespeare), the son of Queen Elizabeth'*. In fact belief regarding Bacon's authorship of the Shakespeare sonnets and plays extends right back to his own lifetime, though this information was suppressed and concealed for many years. Only in Victorian times were his claims to the authorship to be restated.

In this brief account, I shall only have time to sketch in the events and achievements of Bacon's life and little opportunity of including evidence in support of what I shall say.

Fig 2
Princess Elizabeth (1533-1603), aged 14 in 1547

In 1548 Princess Elizabeth, daughter of Henry VIII and Anne Boleyn, aged 14 (Fig 2), was seduced by her guardian Thomas Seymour who had secretly married Catherine Parr following the death of Henry VIII. Elizabeth was strongly rumoured to have had a child by Thomas. Seymour himself (Fig 3) was executed the following year for treason. Following this scandal, Elizabeth lived very quietly during the next decade, much of the time under house arrest during Mary's reign.

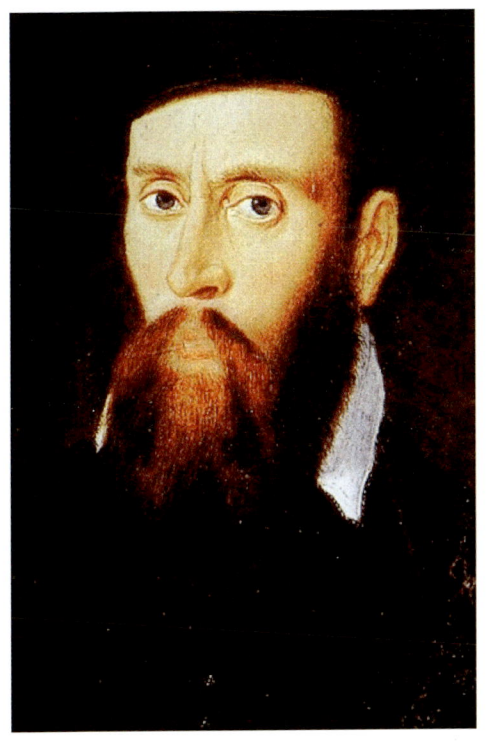

Fig 3
Thomas Seymour, Baron Sudley (1508-1549)

Fig 4
Elizabeth I at her Coronation in 1559

At the age of 25, following Queen Mary's death, Elizabeth came to the throne in 1558 (Fig 4).

*Fig 5
Robert Dudley
Earl of Leicester
(1533-1588)*

One of her first actions was to appoint Robert Dudley, her friend since childhood, to be Master of the Horse (Fig 5). Soon it became apparent to everyone that she was madly in love with him and within a year they were sleeping together. By 1560 she had become pregnant. Conveniently Robert's wife, Amy Robsart, died in September that year. Elizabeth and Robert then

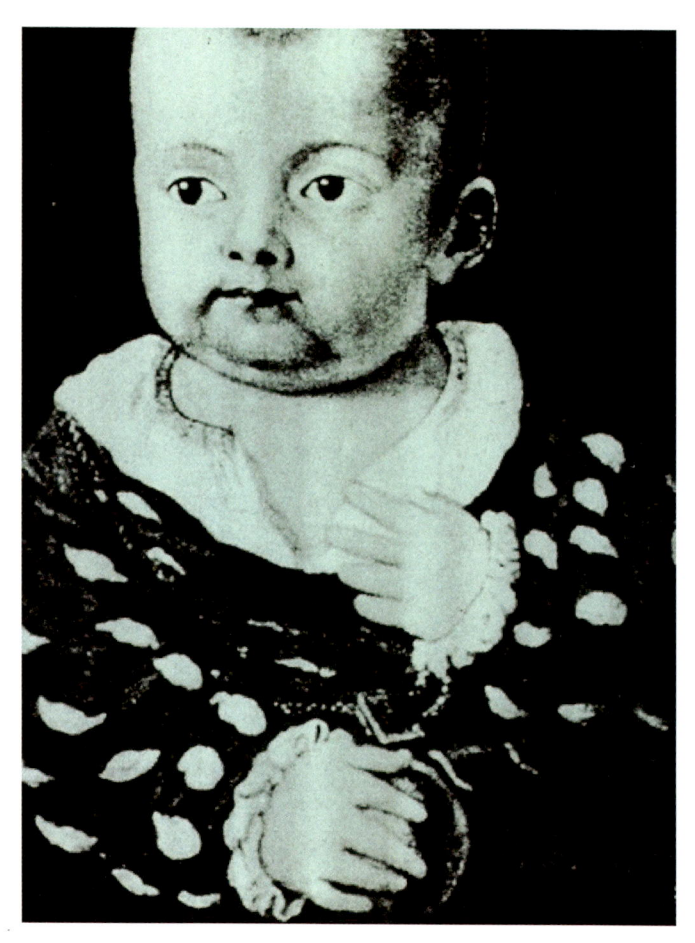

Fig 6
Francis Bacon (1561-1626) in infancy

went through a betrothal ceremony two weeks later in the Earl of Pembroke's house in London, and in January 1561 she gave birth to their son. This boy was fostered with Anne Bacon, Lady of the Bed Chamber, and baptised Francis Bacon (Fig 6). Because Francis was illegitimate and the knowledge of his birth would have ended Elizabeth's reign forthwith, she never publically

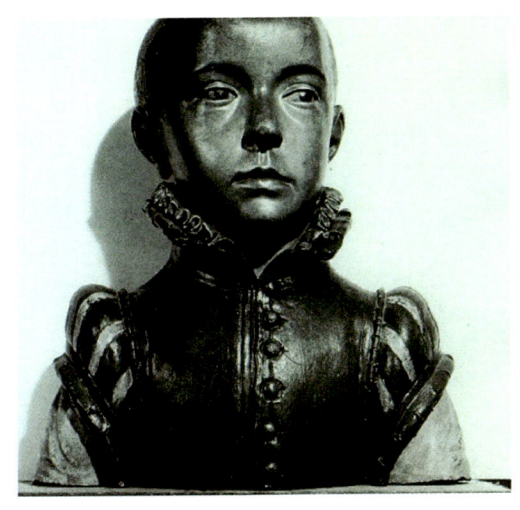

*Fig 7
Francis Bacon
as a young lad.
Terracotta bust.*

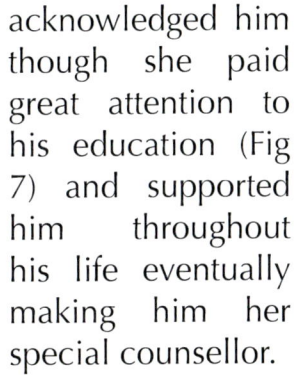

acknowledged him though she paid great attention to his education (Fig 7) and supported him throughout his life eventually making him her special counsellor.

Five years after the birth of Francis, Elizabeth (Fig 8) gave birth to a second son by Robert Dudley that was fostered with her close friend and cousin, Lettice Devereux.

*Fig 8
Queen Elizabeth I
in 1566*

Fig 9
*Portrait of Queen Elizabeth I with her two sons
by Robert Dudley. An infant, possibly her child by Thomas
Seymour may be just made out in the shadows*

Lettice's husband, Walter, was rewarded by being made Earl of Essex, a title that the child, named Robert after his true father, inherited at the age of ten when his foster father Walter died (see frontispiece). Significantly, three years after young Robert's birth, the Queen altered the Act of Succession through Parliament in 1570 to make it an offence to regard any person as heir to the throne other than offspring of her natural body. Previously the Act had read 'legal' offspring.

Returning to Bacon, his birth was a very closely guarded state secret. Those who knew of it kept very quiet if they wished to escape severe retribution. However, censorship was, of course, only effective in England. On the continent, knowledge of Elizabeth's births was widely known. This contemporary painting by a Dutch artist, Van der Werff, shows her with her two children by Robert Dudley (Fig 9). If you peer carefully, you may even see a baby in the shadows on the right possibly representing her child by Thomas Seymour.

Francis's foster parents, the Bacons, were highly educated and he also had the finest tutors. In addition, the Queen arranged for her own favourite tutor, Roger Ascham, to write a book on the education of a young aristocrat; it was called 'The Schoolmaster'. From an early age Francis was recognised as an infant prodigy (Fig 10).

At the age of twelve he was admitted to Trinity College, Cambridge, where he lodged with the Master for the next three years. On coming down at the age of fifteen, he was entered into Gray's Inn to study law.

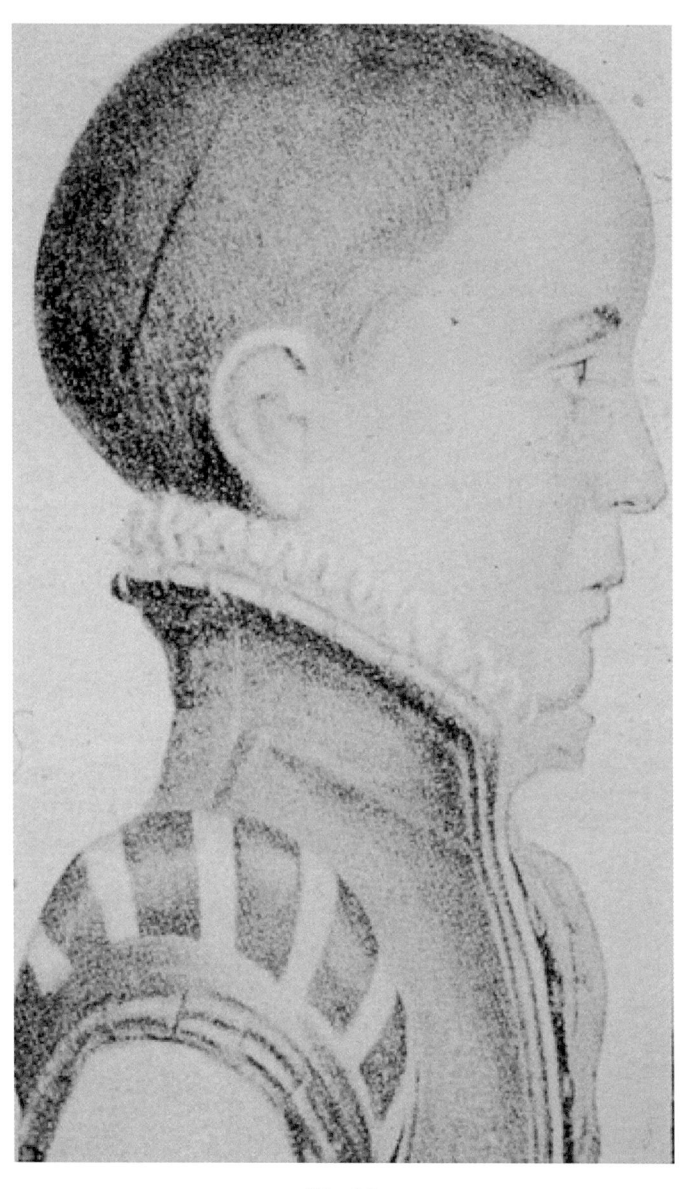

*Fig 10
Francis Bacon, aged 11 years*

At this point in 1576, aged fifteen, Francis discovered by accident that the Queen was his true mother. At once he was withdrawn by her from Gray's Inn after only two months there and packed off in one of the royal warships to the Court of Henry III in France. He was accompanied by his French tutor, Amyas Paulet, knighted for the occasion, and made a supernumerary ambassador to France (Fig 11).

Fig 11
Sir Amyas Paulet (1536-1588),
Ambassador to France, 1576-9

Fig 12
*Pierre de Ronsard (1524-1585),
poet and leader of the Pléiard in France*

In France Bacon travelled widely. He also came at the French Court under the influence of Pierre de Ronsard (Fig 12) who, with a small group of young poets, was attempting to bring the Renaissance from Italy to France. Indeed it was at that time that Bacon conceived the idea of doing the same for England.

*Fig 13
Marguerite de Valois
(1553-1615), aged
c.20,
daughter of Henry II
of France*

Another associate member of this group of poets named the Pléiard was the beautiful and very intelligent Marguerite de Valois, daughter of the late Henry II of France (Fig 13). Francis fell passionately in love with her and it was to her that he wrote some of the loveliest love poems ever written. They appear in altered order among "Shakespeare's" sonnets:

> *'Shall I compare thee to a summer's day?
> Thou art more lovely and more temperate:
> Rough winds do shake the darling buds of May,
> And summer's lease hath all too short a date ...'*

Fig 14
View of the Thames and Richmond Palace in Tudor times

Bacon also wrote one of his earliest plays about Marguerite some ten years later under the title: *'Loves Labour Lost'*. However, Elizabeth put paid to any thought he may have had of marriage to Marguerite.

In 1579, Nicholas Bacon, Francis's foster-father died and Francis, aged eighteen, returned to England. Nicholas had provided generous bequests for all his own seven children but nothing for Francis. The clear implication was that he was the responsibility of his real mother, the Queen. Indeed Elizabeth using indirect methods, gave Francis Twickenham Park with eighty-six acres of land, just across the River Thames from her favourite palace at Richmond (Fig 14).

*Fig 15. Francis Bacon aged 18
Miniature by Hilliyard*

There he created a beautiful garden and also worked for the next twenty years with the help of a team of what he termed his 'good pens', his secretaries. This portrait of Francis by Hilliard, the Royal miniaturist, was painted at this time (Fig 15).

Hilliard commented: *'If only I could paint his mind'.*

Fig 16. Gray's Inn, London in Tudor times

In 1579 Bacon had also returned to his legal studies at Grays Inn (Fig 16) and in 1583 became a barrister. Instead of practicing at the Bar, he then became an unpaid councillor to the Queen.

Only under James I did he rise through the legal ranks to become finally Lord Chancellor in 1618. While at Grays Inn Bacon took a great interest in the production of their annual Christmas plays which were attended by the whole Court. Indeed some of the so-called Shakespeare plays, especially comedies, like the Comedy of Errors, were first performed there.

Fig 17. House of Commons, Queen Elizabeth presiding

In 1584 Bacon entered Parliament (Fig 17). There he quickly established himself as the finest orator in the House of Commons. As a colleague wrote: *'You could hear a pin drop as he rose to speak'*. Soon after his entry to Parliament, he wrote a memorandum to the Queen, bypassing her ministers, on how to solve the many problems confronting the country at that time. He was just twenty-three. Only his close relationship with the Queen would have permitted him to do this.

When eventually, after thirty-six years as a member

of the House, he was ennobled by James in 1618, the Commons successfully petitioned the King to allow him to continue to sit in the House even though now being a member of the Lords. He is the only man ever to have sat simultaneously in both houses. Bacon's statesmanship was revealed over the years in many ways such as by his defence of the common lands, by his insistence that the Commons should control taxation, and by his efforts to unite Scotland with England after James had come to the throne.

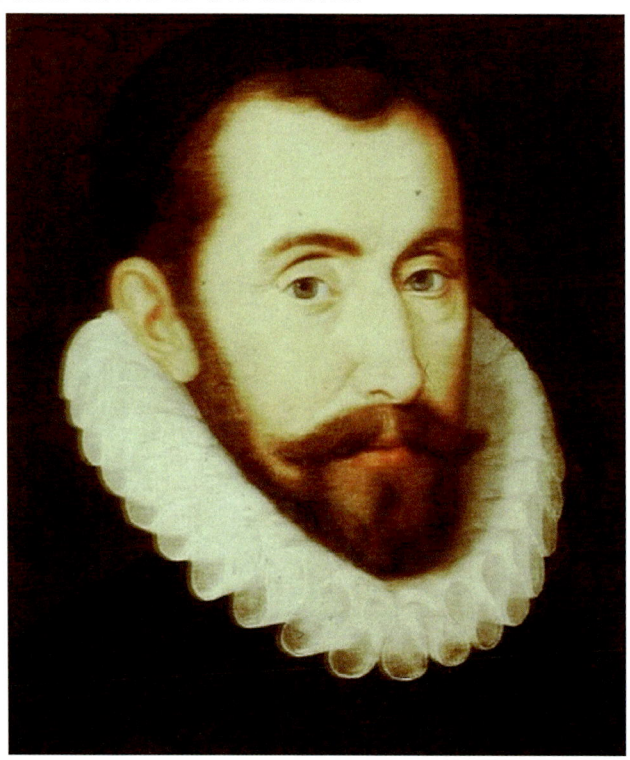

Fig 18. Sir Francis Walsingham (1532-1590) Secretary of State & Spy-master to Elizabeth I

Among Bacon's other activities during the 1580s and 90s was that of working with his foster brother, Anthony, in the Intelligence Service against Spain run by Sir Francis Walsingham (Fig 18). He became an expert in making and breaking cipher codes.

He also resurrected the *'Templers'* (Fig 19) that had been destroyed by Phillip the Fair of France in the 14th century, as a new and secret society termed the Freemasons and became their Grand Master.

Fig 19
The Templar Church, London

As though this was not enough, Francis Bacon also founded yet another secret society of Illuminati named the Rosie-Cross Literary Society. This became the equivalent to the Pléiard in France. He created it in order to assist him bringing the Renaissance to England.

Its members were committed not only to anonymity but to improving and extending the English language besides translating classical and European works into English. Bacon himself (figure 20) has been credited with more than doubling the English vocabulary within his lifetime. Gradually English took over from Latin during the next century.

Fig 20
Sir Francis Bacon (1561-1626)

In 1592 Bacon wrote to William Cecil, his foster uncle: *'I have taken all knowledge to be my province'*. He called his life-long project the Instauratio Magna, a work eventually to be published in six parts, through which he planned to change and improve every aspect of English culture and philosophy. But note that in the whole of Elizabeth's reign only a single book was published under his own name. This was his 'Essays' written in 1597. It was his response to the publication of his friend Montaigne's book of Essays, published in France a few years earlier. Bacon's essays went through four editions during his lifetime and is a remarkable work.

The main reasons for Bacon's insistence on the need for anonymity and his use of numerous non-de-plumes throughout his life may be found in the table below.

REASONS FOR FRANCIS BACON'S DESIRE FOR ANONYMITY

- *His foster father taught him the dangers of writing under his own name.*
- *Though of royal blood, he was a commoner writing about State matters and the Court.*
- *Many of his writings especially his poems were of a very personal nature.*
- *Playwrights and poets were of very low status.*
- *An anonymous message was likely to have a greater impact than that from a commoner.*

Apart from anything else it was extremely dangerous to attach one's name to any written document especially if you were writing about people at Court as he often was in his plays. His Sonnets were also highly personal

Fig 21
Lady Lettice Knollys (1543-1636),
Countess of Essex and later Countess of Leicester

and autobiographical. Having said that, Bacon used a number of devices to identify his own works, one of which I will return to later.

I mentioned that Elizabeth's second child by Robert Dudley had been fostered by her favourite lady of the Privy Chamber, her young cousin Lettice Devereux who was also regarded as the belle of the court (Fig 21).

Robert Dudley had an affair with her in the 1570s

Fig 22
Elizabeth I (1533-1603).
The Armada Portrait

and when she became pregnant, secretly (probably bigamously) married her in 1578 (see frontispiece). The Queen only found out about this two years later and was absolutely furious. But her hands were tied. While Robert was eventually forgiven, Lettice was banished from the Court for the remainder of the Queen's reign.

In 1588 the Spanish Armada was defeated (Fig 22) and one month later Robert Dudley died of stomach problems at the age of fifty-five.

Fig 23
Robert Devereux, 2nd Earl of Essex as a young man

The Queen was heartbroken. She actually referred at the time to Robert as her *'erstwhile husband'* and dealt with all his possessions as though being his wife and next of kin, ignoring Lettice.

Some four years before his death Robert Dudley had introduced their second son, Robert Devereux, aged eighteen and now Earl of Essex (Fig 23), to Court. Dudley persuaded the Queen to make him her Master of the Horse in place of himself. After Dudley's death

Fig 24
Henry Wriothesley, 3rd Earl of Southampton, aged 21

she also gave young Robert the rooms next to hers that his father had previously occupied. The Queen spent much of her time alone in the evenings and late into the night with Essex. Some thought he was her toy-boy but she was, I believe, training him in statecraft with a view to his being her eventual successor.

Meanwhile, the young 3rd Earl of Southampton, Henry Wriothesly (Fig 24) had become a ward of William Cecil on the death of his immensely rich father,

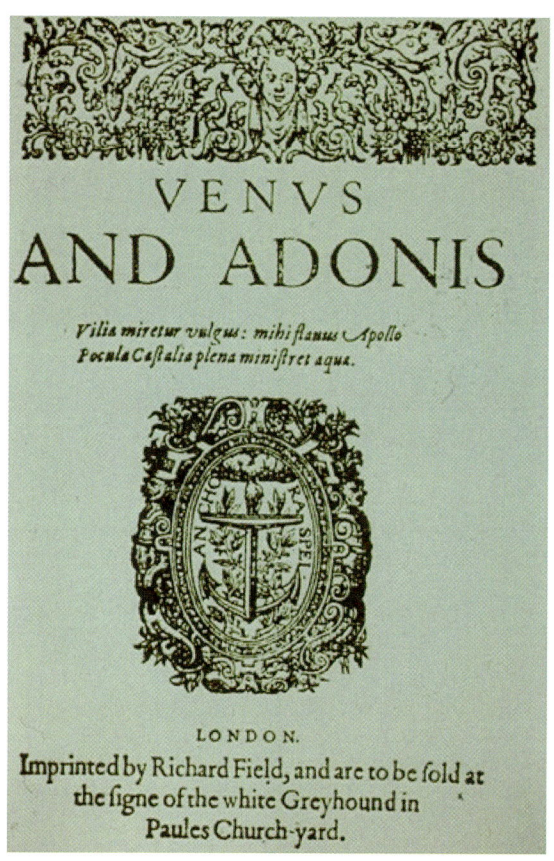

Fig 25
*Frontpiece to the poem Venus and Adonis
by 'William Shakespeare', 1593,
printed by Richard Field, St. Paul's Churchyard*

the second Earl. Cecil entered him to Gray's Inn to study law and asked Francis Bacon to keep an eye on him. This Bacon did and they became great friends. In 1593 young Southampton celebrated his twenty-first birthday. Bacon wrote and dedicated a poem to him, 'Venus and Adonis' (Fig 25). Please note the name of the printer, Richard Field. He was the owner of a

34

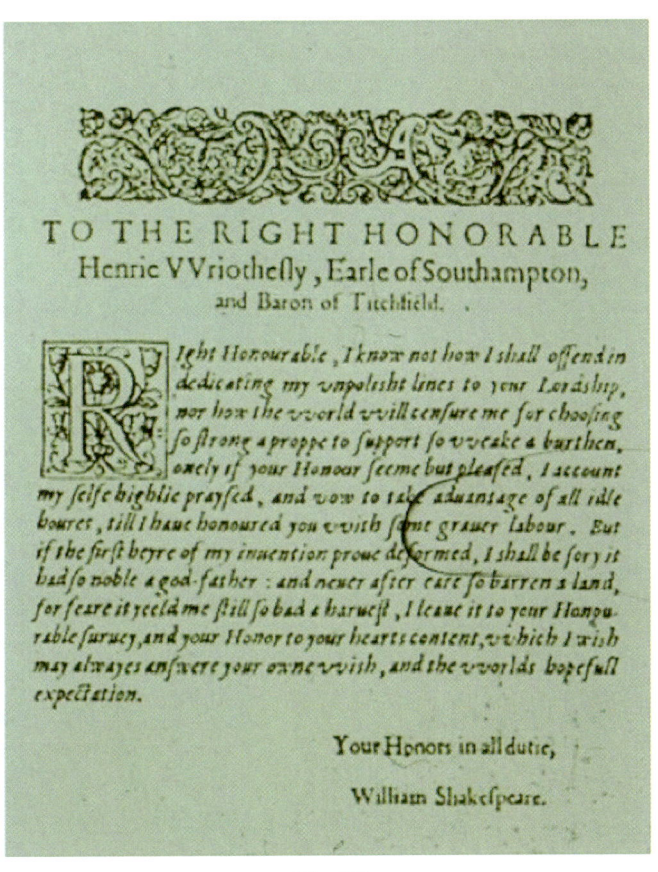

Fig 26
Dedication of Venus and Adonis to Henry Wriothesly,
3rd Earl of Southampton, 1593

bookshop in Old St. Paul's, London. Field had been born in Stratford upon Avon and was a contemporary and friend of one William Shagspur, a small time actor who now lived nearby in Silver Street. Field was also the printer regularly used by Bacon in the 1590s.

Accompanying the poem by Bacon to Southampton was a letter signed "William Shakespeare" (Fig 26).

Fig 27
Pallas Athena, the Goddess of Wisdom in Ancient Greece

This was the first time Bacon had used this non-de-plume. Notice the wood cut over the letter with its dark and light As. This and other wood cuts belonged to Bacon and it was his practice to lend them briefly to printers when he wished to record his own secret authorship of a work that they were printing.

Let me explain the two As – the dark A indicating ignorance and the light A indicating knowledge. The A stood for Pallas Athena (Fig 27), the Greek Goddess of Wisdom that Bacon had adopted as his muse. She was also known in classical times as 'the Speare-shaker'. Small wonder it appealed to Bacon's sense of humour to use the name William Shakespeare as his non-de-plume.

I should also mention that Bacon named all the anonymous Illuminati of the Rosie-Cross Literary Society as his 'Knights of the Helmet' – Pallas Athene's helmet. By the way, William is the German for helmet.

As I have mentioned there was a small time actor at the Theatre in north London, called William Shagspur. Very little is known about his life except that he was born in Stratford-on-Avon, was a friend of Richard Field, also born in Stratford, had married the already pregnant Anne Hathaway at the age of eighteen, and had then deserted her and their three children leaving her in poverty when for ten years he disappeared to London.

He was not a very admirable character but became wealthy at the age of thirty-four when paid to adopt the authorship of the *"Shakespeare plays and sonnets"* as his own. We even know what he looked like for this is the original bust of him in Trinity Church, Stratford (Fig 28). It was recorded in this etching in Sir William Dugdale's book on Warwickshire (1630) soon after Shagspur's death. Note that he is clutching a sack of corn. In Stratford he was known only as a corn merchant and money lender.

Fig 28
The bust of William Shagspur in Trinity Church, Stratford on Avon, taken from an etching in Sir. William Dugdale's book on Warwickshire in 1630

Fig 29
The present bust of William Shakespeare in Trinity Church, Stratford on Avon, probably raised in the 1740s

Fig 30 Six signatures of William Shagspur taken from legal documents, 1612-1616

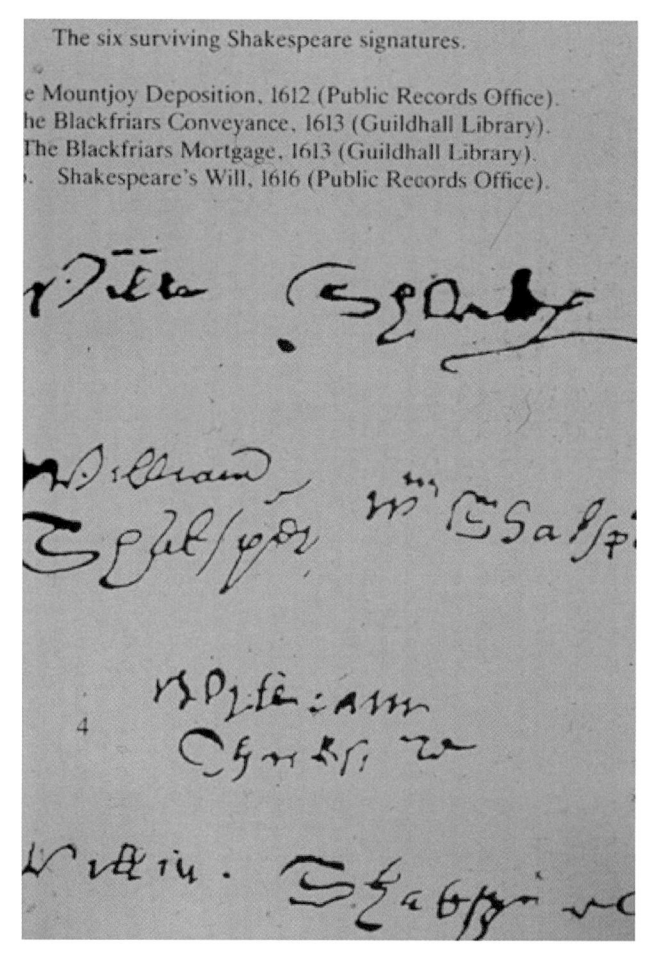

The six surviving Shakespeare signatures.

e Mountjoy Deposition, 1612 (Public Records Office).
he Blackfriars Conveyance, 1613 (Guildhall Library).
The Blackfriars Mortgage, 1613 (Guildhall Library).
Shakespeare's Will, 1616 (Public Records Office).

The present image in Trinity Church of Shakespeare or Shagspur (Fig 29) is very different from the one that it replaced 125 years later in the 1740s when the Shakespeare plays were being resurrected and the myths on their authorship were being reinvented by David Garrick and others.

You will notice the learned features of the 'new' Shakespeare and the paper and pen in his hands. In fact the evidence is that William Shagspur was illiterate, like

Fig 31
William Shagspur's birthplace in Stratford on Avon, destroyed in the 18th century

his father John before him, and also his three children. No books, paper or pens were found in his home after his death and the only words that have ever been found written by him are these six crude signatures on legal documents (Fig 30).

Certainly no one in Stratford ever credited him with being a poet or playwright during his life or in the years soon after his death. Yet the myth that the Stratford man had written the finest poems and plays of all time persists and is very fiercely defended. Woe betide anyone who challenges his authorship. Of course, apart from habit, an enormous amount of intellectual and commercial investment depends on keeping that myth alive. For example, William Shakespeare's birthplace (Fig 31) was actually destroyed two hundred years ago. Yet a house in Stratford described as his place of birth brings in more than ten million pounds each year.

Now please compare Bacon's hand writing (Fig 32) with that of Shagspur's signatures.

At this point I should also mention Bacon's *'Promus'* or storehouse of memorable sayings. He produced many folios of these sayings over the years but almost all were deliberately destroyed during his lifetime. By chance those for the years 1594-96 survived and are currently held in the British Museum. They are in Bacon's handwriting and are written in English, French, Latin or Greek.

They are full of phrases that he used later, both in his own works and also in those published under the Shakespeare non-de-plume. Let me give you a few examples:

'One swallow maketh no summer'.
'To leap out of the frying pan into the fire'.
'Two eyes are better than one'.
'All is not gold that glistens'.
'Pride will have a fall'.

While the average educated person in Bacon's day had an English vocabulary of around 4000 words, Bacon had one of more than 20,000. Nor can it be a coincidence to learn that the *'Shakespeare's works'* also contain 20,000 different words.

I should point out that plays were an important means at that time of communicating with the population that was still mainly illiterate.

During the late 1580s and early 1590s at least a dozen plays that subsequently appeared in the Shakespeare

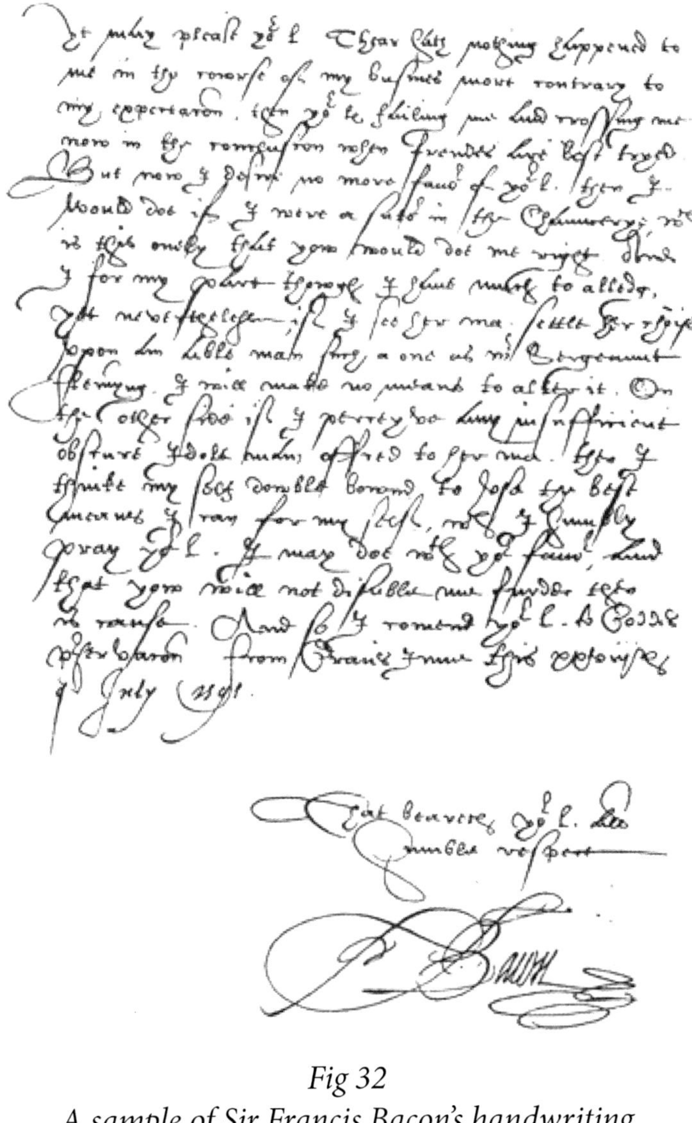

It may please yor l. There hath nothing happened to
me in the course of my business more contrary to
my expectacon, then yor l. failing me and crossing me
now in the conclusion when frends are best tryed.
But now I desire no more favor of yor l. then I
would doe if I were a suto[illegible] in the Chauncery, wch
is this only, that you would doe me right. And
I for my part though I have much to allege,
yet neverthelesse if I see her ma. settle her choyse
upon an hable man such a one as mr Sergeant
Fleming, I will make no meanes to alter it. On
the other side if I perceyve any insufficient
obscure idole man offred to her ma. then I
think my self double bound to use the best
meanes I can for my self, wch I humbly
pray yor l. I may doe wth yor favor, and
that you will not disable me further then
is cause. And so I commend yor l. to Godds
preservacon. From Graies Inne this [illegible]
[illegible] July [illegible].

That beareth yor l. all
humble respect

Fr. Bacon

Fig 32
A sample of Sir Francis Bacon's handwriting

THE
Tragedie of King Richard the second.

As it hath beene publikely acted by the right Honourable the Lorde Chamberlaine his Seruants.

LONDON
Printed by Valentine Simmes for Androw Wife, and are to be sold at his shop in Paules church yard at the signe of the Angel.

Fig 33
Frontispiece of 'The Tragedie of King Richard II' c.1597
Note the absence of authorship

Fig 34
Robert Devereaux, Earl of Essex and
Marshall of England (1597)

First Folio had been published without a named author, like this one on Richard II (Fig 33). (Note that this play could be purchased at Richard Field's bookshop in Old St. Paul's.) In around 1598 all these anonymous plays, when reprinted, had acquired the name of an author, William Shakespeare.

Fig 35
Queen Elizabeth I portrayed shortly before her death in 1603

How did this come about? Well, Essex, Elizabeth's second son by Robert Dudley, had risen to become next to the Queen at Court and Marshall of all England (Fig 34).

He had every reason to believe that he would eventually succeed her. Unfortunately, from 1595, they had begun increasingly to quarrel. Eventually he wished that she would abdicate in his favour. In 1600 he arranged for the play Richard II to be played at the Globe Theatre. It was about the forced abdication of an earlier monarch. The following day he led an attempted coup to take over the Government. The coup failed and he was executed soon afterwards within the Tower of London, something significantly that was only permitted for those of royal blood. All others were executed outside on Tower Green.

When the Queen had first seen the play Richard II in 1598, two years before the attempted coup, she said: *'Know thee not, that is me?'* pointing at Richard II. She added: *'Find the playwright and we will rack the truth out of him'*. This at once led for Bacon's need to find a non-de-plume for Richard II and the other previously published anonymous plays. It was at this time too that William Shagspur left his address in north London in a hurry without paying his taxes and lost himself in the shady stews of Southwark, south of the Thames.

Meanwhile the Queen became increasingly melancholic (Fig 35) and, three years later, refusing to eat, drink or confess, died at the age of seventy.

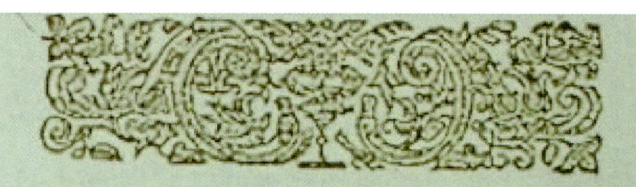

The Tragicall Historie of
HAMLET
Prince of Denmarke.

Enter two Centinels.

1. Stand: who is that?
2. Tis I.
1. O you come most carefully vpon your watch,
2. And if you meete *Marcellus* and *Horatio*,
The partners of my watch, bid them make haste.
1. I will: See who goes there.

Enter Horatio and Marcellus.

Hor. Friends to this ground.
Mar. And leegemen to the Dane,
O farewell honest fouldier, who hath releeued you?
1. *Bernardo* hath my place, giue you good night.
Mar. Holla, *Bernardo*.
2. Say, is *Horatio* there?
Hor. A peece of him.
2. Welcome *Horatio*, welcome good *Marcellus*.
Mar. What hath this thing appear'd againe to night.
2. I haue seene nothing.
Mar. *Horatio* sayes tis but our fantasie,
And wil not let beliefe take hold of him,
Touching this dreaded sight twice seene by vs,

B   There-

Fig 36
Frontispiece of the Tragicall Historie of Hamlet by William Shakespeare, 1601. Note the double As in the woodcut

Francis Bacon, who was of course the brother of Robert, Earl of Essex, was equally devastated by Robert's death and wrote the first of his tragedies, Hamlet, the same year, 1601 (Fig 36 - Please note the double A's in the woodcut.) It is full of hidden references to the terrible events that had just taken place. Later it was followed by other tragedies such as Othello, Macbeth and King Lear.

Following Elizabeth's death in 1603, James VI of Scotland came to the throne as James I of England (Fig 37). Francis Bacon, being of royal blood, realised that his life was at great risk. He travelled north to meet James on his way south and persuaded him that he had no aspirations to the throne. To prove the point he agreed to marry a commoner. This he did in 1606 by marrying a young girl of fourteen, Alice Barnham. He was thirty years older than her and it is likely that they did not live as man and wife. A significant fact requires mention. At their wedding, Francis dressed himself in purple, a colour that had been strictly reserved for royalty by decree by his grandfather, Henry VIII. In fact later he was to repeat this act when James elevated him to the nobility in 1618. Meantime, the King over the years employed him successively as Solicitor General, Auditor General, Keeper of the Seal, and Lord Chancellor. Then in 1617 while James spent several months in Scotland, Bacon was actually appointed Regent of England in his place.

Fig 37
King James I of England (1566-1625)

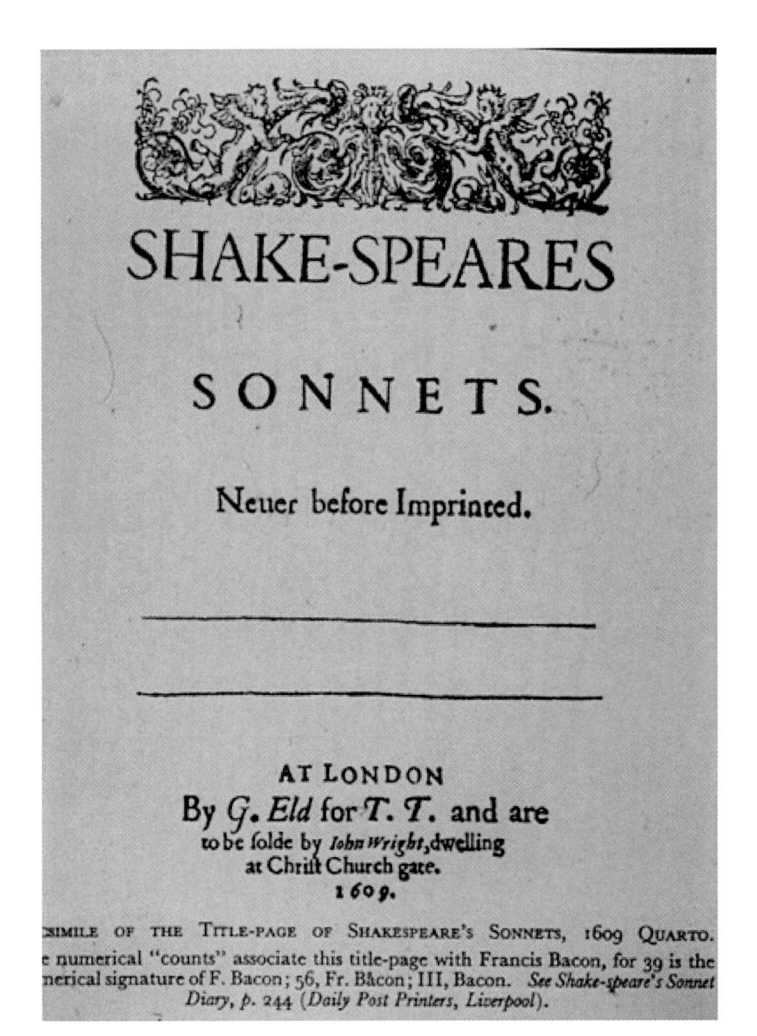

> # SHAKE-SPEARES
>
> ## SONNETS.
>
> Neuer before Imprinted.
>
> ---
>
> ---
>
> AT LONDON
> By G. Eld for T. T. and are
> to be folde by *Iohn Wright*, dwelling
> at Chrift Church gate.
> 1609.
>
> :SIMILE OF THE TITLE-PAGE OF SHAKESPEARE'S SONNETS, 1609 QUARTO.
> e numerical "counts" associate this title-page with Francis Bacon, for 39 is the
> nerical signature of F. Bacon; 56, Fr. Bãcon; III, Bacon. *See Shake-speare's Sonnet
> Diary, p.* 244 (*Daily Post Printers, Liverpool*).

Fig 38
Frontispiece of Shake-speare's Sonnets, 1609

In 1609 Bacon had registered his sonnets with the Stationer, though only after altering the order in which they had been written (Fig 38). They were indeed very personal and autobiographical. Though a limited edition was circulated among close friends in 1625, they were

51

SHAKE-SPEARES, SONNETS.

FRom fairest creatures we desire increase,
 That thereby beauties Rose might neuer die,
But as the riper should by time decease,
His tender heire might beare his memory:
But thou contracted to thine owne bright eyes,
Feed'st thy lights flame with selfe substantiall fewell,
Making a famine where aboundance lies,
Thy selfe thy foe,to thy sweet selfe too cruell:
Thou that art now the worlds fresh ornament,
And only herauld to the gaudy spring,
Within thine owne bud buriest thy content,
And tender chorle makst wast in niggarding:
  Pitty the world,or else this glutton be,
  To eate the worlds due,by the graue and thee.

2

VVHen fortie Winters shall beseige thy brow,
 And digge deep trenches in thy beauties field,
Thy youthes proud liuery so gaz'd on now,
Wil be a totter'd weed of smal worth held:
Then being askt,where all thy beautie lies,
Where all the treasure of thy lusty daies;
To say within thine owne deepe sunken eyes,
Were an all-eating shame,and thriftlesse praise.
How much more praise deseru'd thy beauties vse,
If thou couldst answere this faire child of mine
Shall sum my count,and make my old excuse
Proouing his beautie by succession thine.

Fig 39
Shake-speare's Sonnets. Note the double As in the woodcut

only published in 1641, fifteen years after his death. The reason he had registered them in 1609 was because some of them had been stolen and pirated. I include a

Fig 40
Princess Elizabeth, daughter of James I at the time of her marriage to the Elector of the Paletine in 1613

page from the original printing (Fig 39) to demonstrate that above the title of Shakespeare's Sonnets, is again the wooden bookcut with Bacon's double A's. The same wooden bookcut may also be found on the original first 1611 edition of the King James' Bible.

In 1613 King James' daughter, Princess Elizabeth (Fig 40), married the Elector of the Palentine. The

*Fig 41
Frontispiece
of Sir Francis
Bacon's
'Advancement
and Proficience
of Learning' of
the Partitions
of Science*

King laid on great celebrations and put Francis Bacon in charge of them. Indeed it was at this time that Francis prepared the play on his grandfather, Henry VIII. Subsequently, with significant alterations, it was included in the First Folio of the Shakespeare plays.

Meanwhile Bacon had been steadily working on his great project to improve every aspect of English

*Fig 42
Frontispiece
of 'Novum
Organum' by Sir
Francis Bacon,
1620*

philosophy and culture. Here is the title page of his 'Advancement and Proficience of Learning of the Partitions of Science' (Fig 41) and here is that of his Novum Organum published in 1620 (Fig 42). Perhaps most importantly he taught that we should put behind us all the reliance that had been placed on ancient writings such as those of Aristotle, Galen and others and learn instead from observation, experiment and deduction, based on facts.

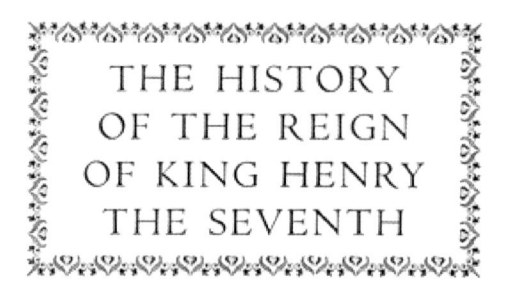

Fig 43
Frontispiece of Sir Francis Bacon's 'History of the Reign of Henry the Seventh', 1621

Francis Bacon

THE HISTORY
OF THE REIGN
OF KING HENRY
THE SEVENTH

*Edited
with an Introduction
by Roger Lockyer*

LONDON
THE FOLIO SOCIETY
MCMLXXI

At this time he also published under his own name *'The Reign of Henry VII'* (Fig 43) in prose rather than as a play, thus completing his series of English Kings from King John up to Henry VIII, a subject that naturally was of great interest to Bacon, being of royal blood himself. Why was it in prose? Well, his non-de-plume, William Shagspur, had died in 1616, uncelebrated and indeed virtually unnoticed at the time. It was of interest to me that Roger Lockyer, the Editor of the Folio edition of Henry VII and not himself a Baconian, wrote in his preface: *'Bacon's style can embrace with equal felicity*

Fig 44
Sir Edward Coke (1552-1634),
a great lawyer but a foe of Sir Francis Bacon

the long Latinised sentence or the brief pithy epigram ... when occasion requires Bacon can write in a way that recalls Shakespeare'.

In 1621 when Francis was at the height of his career, his nemesis Sir Edward Coke, engineered a conspiracy that brought about his disgrace and downfall.

Coke (Fig 44) while being a great lawyer and also Speaker of the House of Commons, was a very nasty piece of work and loathed Bacon. His animosity, both personal and professional, dated back thirty years to the early 1590s. He and his conspirators achieved

Fig 45
George Villiers, 1st Duke of Buckingham
(1592-1628), favourite of James I

Bacon's downfall by threatening to prosecute the King's favourite, George Villiers, the Duke of Buckingham (Fig 45), over abuse of the monopolies unless the King gave them Bacon instead. As a result, Bacon was requested by the King to plead guilty to charges of bribery and corruption. This with reluctance he did. Bacon was then removed from office as Lord Chancellor and forbidden to reside in London.

Fig 46
Gorhambury House, the Bacon family home

In retrospect, his downfall can in fact be seen as a blessing in disguise. Bacon withdrew to his foster-father's old home, Gorhambury, near St. Albans (Fig 46) and concentrated on trying to complete his great project, the 'Instauratio Magna'.

With the help of a team of 'good pens' including the poet laureate, Ben Jonson (Fig 47), Bacon produced a prodigious number of works, many of them being published after his death, including 'New Atlantis' on how a country might be best governed.

Fig 47
Ben Jonson (1573-1637), poet and dramatist

Mr. WILLIAM
SHAKESPEARES
COMEDIES,
HISTORIES, &
TRAGEDIES.

Published according to the True Originall Copies.

LONDON
Printed by Isaac Iaggard, and Ed. Blount. 1623.

Fig 48
Martin Droeshout's engraving of William Shakespeare in the First Folio of the Shakespeare plays published in 1623

Most important of all, in 1623 he published the First Folio of the thirty-six "Shakespeare" plays (Fig 48).

Eighteen of these plays had not appeared before in print. Many of them had been significantly revised and improved prior to their inclusion. I hardly need to remind you that William Shagspur had been in his grave for the last seven years.

Fig 49
Portrait of Sir Francis Bacon (left) compared with the Droeshout etching of William Shakespeare in the First Folio of the Shakespeare plays (1623)

The engraving of "William Shakespeare", the <u>only</u> likeness in existence, is very different to that of the original bust of William Shagspur in Trinity Church that I showed earlier (Fig 28). However, it has a remarkable resemblance to that of Francis Bacon on which I believe it was based. Here you see both portraits together to ease comparison (Fig 49). It would be typical of Bacon's wit to use his own likeness to portray his non-de-plume. He was a disgraced and very elderly man and perhaps cared less if the truth finally became known.

Bacon practised other illusions, again typical of his wit and love of mystery. Ben Jonson, in his Foreword to the First Folio, speaks of Stratford-upon-Avon and for four hundred years we have all assumed he was

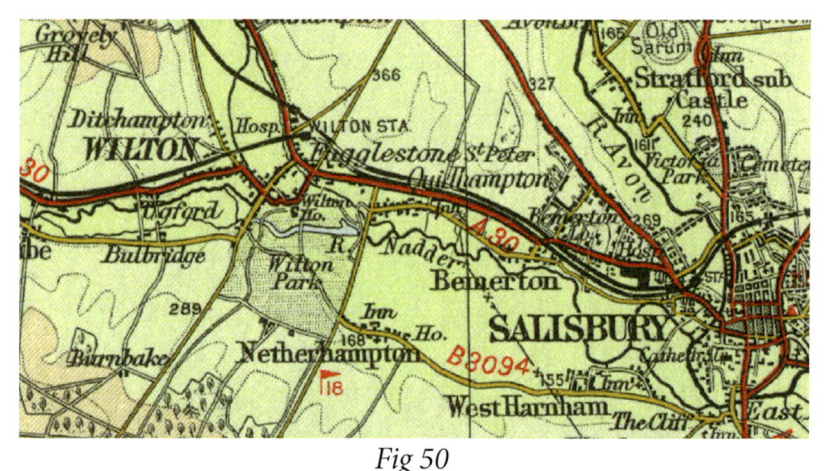

Fig 50
An old map of the area around Salisbury, Wiltshire showing Wilton, home of the Earl of Pembroke, the River Avon and the village of Stratford

referring to the town in Warwickshire. But in fact, there are eight River Avons in England and Bacon, through Ben Jonson, was actually alluding to the Stratford-on-Avon in Wiltshire (Fig 50). This Stratford lies next door to Wilton, the home of the Earl of Pembroke, to whom the First Folio was dedicated as 'WH' or William Herbert (Fig 51). He was at the time Lord Chamberlain to King James.

Fig 51. William Herbert, 3rd Earl of Pembroke (1580-1630), Lord Chamberlain to James I

62

Fig 52
Mary Herbert, Countess of Pembroke (1561-1621)

William's wife, Mary Herbert, Countess of Pembroke (Fig 52) and a cousin of Francis Bacon, was referred to by Jonson as the 'Sweet Swan of Avon'. She was a fine poet in her own right. Once again, Bacon must be laughing in his grave at the notion that the coarse man in the bust in Trinity Church had been alluded to in those terms for four hundred years.

In 2004 Peter Dawkins, Shakespearean critic to the Globe, published an excellent book entitled *'The Shakespeare Enigma'*. Here is an extract from his book. Based on the Shakespeare writings, he wrote:

'The evidence of the plays is that the true author of Shakespeare was someone who was not only exceptionally inspired and talented, but well educated, someone who loved reading, had access to a wide range of books and manuscripts, written in classical, foreign and English languages (some of them extremely rare), and who possessed an extraordinary mind and memory capable of acquiring and retaining an encyclopaedic knowledge.

He was a celebrated philosopher, famous as such in his own lifetime, a supreme poet and initiate of the Mystery teachings, a classical scholar of high standing, able to read and write Latin and Greek with facility, an alumnus of Cambridge University, a lawyer and member of Gray's Inn, a renowned orator, a judge, a parliamentarian and statesman, a courtier, a naturalist or horticulturist, a visitor to various countries and courts of Europe and above all, a master of the English language as well as a multi-linguist, fluent in French, Italian and Spanish.'

A little further on, Dawkins wrote as follows:

'Francis Bacon (Fig 53) was born in 1561 and died in 1626. He was an alumnus of Cambridge University, a classical scholar in Latin, Greek and Hebrew, a multi-linguist fluent in French, Italian and Spanish, an international traveller, a courtier, intelligencer and cryptologist, a celebrated philosopher and writer, a musician, a mystic, a naturalist and horticulturist, a lawyer and barrister. He became in his lifetime a Reader

Fig 53
Statue of Sir Francis Bacon (1561-1626) at Gray's Inn, London

and Treasurer of Gray's Inn, a Member of Parliament, a statesman and, ultimately, as Lord Chancellor, a judge.

He was in addition a renowned orator, poet and playwright who was the acknowledged leader of the poets and wits of his time, and who ran a scrivenery of writers, poets, translators, cryptanalysts and secretaries to assist him. He had a powerful motive for writing the Shakespeare plays as well as being fully capable of doing so. He had the time in which to write them, and the necessary assistance. Moreover, he was alive and of writing age throughout the whole 'Shakespeare' period, from the first appearance of the plays to their *final compilation in the 1623 Shakespeare Folio, in which are certain additions and alterations that could not have been made earlier. He also had more than one good reason to keep his name secret as the author of the Shakespeare poems and plays ...'*

The claims of William Shagspur of Stratford to be the author of the Shakespeare sonnets and plays are compared in the table opposite with those of Francis Bacon.

In October 2016 a headline appeared in the Times: **'Marlowe will share equal credit with Shakespeare'.** The statement was based on the conclusion of a team of international scholars. I was particularly interested as for many years I had been impressed by the similarity of the style, phrasing and use of words of the two playwrights. Indeed seven years ago I suggested to Peter Dawkins when I visited him at his home near Stratford, that Marlowe might have been the first non-de-plume for Bacon's early plays.

Christopher Marlowe (Fig 54) was, of course, murdered in April 1593 in a pub in Deptford. Just one month later, Bacon

Fig 54. Possible portrait of Christopher Marlowe (1564-1593)

The claims of William Shagspur of Stratford and Francis Bacon to be the author of the plays and sonnets published under the name of W. Shakespeare

Characteristics, expertise, knowledge or skill	William Shagspur of Stratford	Francis Bacon
Education, scholarship	No evidence	The very best
Knowledge of classics	No evidence	Expert
Knowledge of French, Italian, Spanish and those countries	No evidence	Yes
Genius, polymath, original thinker	No evidence	Yes
Philosopher	No evidence	Yes
Wit and sense of humour	No evidence	Yes
Legal expertise	No evidence	Yes
Knowledge of Court and Royalty	No evidence	Yes
Knowledge of history	No evidence	Yes
Writer, playwright, poet	"Yes"	Yes
Knowledge of plants and gardens	No evidence	Yes
Attitude to war, love	No evidence	'Shakespearean'
Attitude to religion	No evidence	'Shakespearean'
Use of metaphors, aphorisms	No evidence	'Shakespearean'
Possession of books	No evidence	Yes
Interest in American colonies	No evidence	Yes
Handwriting evidence	No evidence	Yes
Promus evidence	-	Yes
Evidence of Shakespearean scholarship after 1616	-	Yes

Table: The comparison of the claims of William Shagspur of Stratford and Francis Bacon to be the author of the plays and sonnets published under the name of William Shakespeare

used the non-de-plume "William Shakespeare", for the first time in his letter to the young Earl of Southampton accompanying the poem 'Venus and Adonis'. With Marlowe's death, Bacon would have needed to find a new non-de-plume for his poems and plays. Dawkins was sceptical but I think the close timing of these two events must have been more than a coincidence.

Bacon lived to see all the conspirators who had engineered his downfall themselves disgraced. In 1626 he died of pneumonia at the age of sixty-five. In spite of his own so-called 'disgrace', all the leading luminaries, poets and playwrights of his day wrote eulogies to his memory, many more than the thirty-two that could be included in the book of praise dedicated to him after his death.

In his Will, Bacon emphasised that he left it to foreign nations and to future generations to seek the truth about his life. In the years that followed he was widely acknowledged as the greatest thinker and poet of all time. And when, forty years later, the Royal Society was founded in the 1660s he was celebrated as the inspiration for that famous body. In the frontispiece of the first history written about the Royal Society Bacon may be seen sitting by the bust of Charles II (Fig 55). Already acknowledged as the father of modern scientific method he was, I believe the greatest Englishman of his age, if not of all time.

Fig 55
Frontispiece to the History of the Royal Society (1668). Francis Bacon may be seen sitting to the right of the bust of Charles II

A Brief Bibliography

- **Bacon, Francis.** The works of Francis Bacon in ten volumes. W. Baynes and Sons, London, 1824.
- **Bacon, Francis.** The history of the reign of King Henry VII. Folio Society, London, 1971.
- **Bacon, Francis.** Essays. Dent and Sons, London, 1972.
- **Dawkins, Peter.** The Shakespeare Enigma. London: Polair Publ., 2004.
- **Dodd, Alfred.** The personal poems of Francis Bacon. Daily Post Printers, Liverpool, 6th ed. 1938.
- **Dodd, Alfred.** Francis Bacon's personal life story. Rider and Co., London, 1949.
- **du Maurier.** The winding stair. Francis Bacon his rise and fall. Book Club, Camelot Press, Southampton, 1976.
- **Durning-Lawrence, Sir E.** Bacon is Shakespeare Kessinger Publ., USA, 1912.
- **Fields, B.** Players. The mysterious identity of Shakespeare, Harper Collins, New York, 2005.
- **Fuller, Jean Overton.** Sir Francis Bacon. East-West Publ., London, 1981.
- **Hepworth-Dixon, William.** Personal history of Lord Bacon. John Murray, London, 1861.
- **Hilton, D.** Who was Kit Marlowe? Taplinger Publishing Co. Inc., New York, 1977.

- **Jardine, L. & Stewart, A**. Hostage to fortune. The troubled life of Francis Bacon, 1561 – 1626. Phoenix Press, London, 1998.
- **Michell, J.** Who wrote Shakespeare? London: Thames & Hudson, 1996.
- **Montaine, Michel de.** Essays. Penguin Books, Harmondsworth, Middlesex, 1958.
- **Shakespeare, William.** The complete works. Collins, London, 1960.
- **Shapiro, James**. Contested Will. London, Faber & Faber, 2010.

The Bristol Medico-Historical Society

This book is published as a supplement to Volume Eight of the Proceedings of the Bristol Medico-Historical Society.

Officers of the Society

- *President: Lois M. Tutton BDS, MSc.*
- *Hon. Treasurer: Dr. Michael Whitfield*
- *Hon. Secretary: Dr. Peter Carpenter*
- *Hon. Editor: Professor Paul R. Goddard*

About the author

Peter MacNaughton Dunn was born in Birmingham in 1929. He qualified in medicine at the University of Cambridge in 1953. Forging a career in a new specialty, perinatal medicine, he honed his analytical skills on the problems of childbirth and the adaptation of the fetus to extrauterine life. Between 1968 and 1991 he supervised the academic neonatal service of the University of Bristol. In 1976 he founded and was the first president of the Brtitish Association of Perinatal Medicine.

Following retirement he developed a long held interest in the history of perinatal medicine. In 2002 he founded and was president of the British Society for the History of Paediatrics and Child Health. At this time he also became keenly interested in the life of Sir Francis Bacon and the Tudor and Stuart times in which Bacon lived. This very brief account was given as the Christmas lecture to the Bristol Medico-Historical Society in December 2017. Currently he lives with his wife, Judy, in Henbury, Bristol.